also by chris wind

Thus Saith Eve

UnMythed

Deare Sister

The Lady Doth Indeed Protest

Snow White Gets Her Say

Satellites Out of Orbit

Particivision and other stories

Paintings and Sculptures

Excerpts

dreaming

of

kaleidoscopes

dreaming of kaleidoscopes

chris wind

Magenta

Published by Magenta

Magenta

dreaming of kaleidoscopes
© 1991, 2011 by chris wind

ISBN 978-1-926891-13-2

All rights reserved. Without limiting the rights under copyright reserved above, no part of this publication may be reproduced, stored in or introduced into a retrieval system, or transmitted, in any form, or by any means (electronic, mechanical, photocopying, recording, or otherwise) without the prior written permission of both the copyright owner and the above publisher of this book.

This is a work of fiction. Names, characters, places, brands, media, and incidents are either the product of the author's imagination or are used fictitiously. The author acknowledges the trademarked status and trademark owners of various products referenced in this work of fiction, which have been used without permission. The publication/use of these trademarks is not authorized, associated with, or sponsored by the trademark owners.

www.chriswind.net

Cover design by chris wind
Formatting and layout design by Elizabeth Beeton

Cover image by H. Pellikka, used in accordance with the
GNU Free Documentation License, Version 1.2 and
Creative Commons Attribution-Share Alike 2.0
Generic and Unreported licenses

Library and Archives Canada Cataloguing in Publication

Wind, Chris
  Dreaming of kaleidoscopes / Chris Wind.

Poems.
ISBN 978-1-926891-13-2

I. Title.

PS8595.I592D74 2011   C811'.54   C2010-907133-6

acknowledgements

"crease, flip" *Canadian Woman Studies* Spring 98, vol.18 no.1
"Modern Math" (a series) *White Wall Review* 1998, no.23
"Blacks founded..." *Kola* Spring 96, vol.8 no.1; *Onionhead* Jul94, no.24
"stranding" ("it's like a hunger strike") *Bogg* Winter 95, no.67
"in the night" *Shard* Summer 95; *The Free Verse Anthology* Aug93
"To My Philosophy Professors" *Canadian Woman Studies* Winter 94, vol.15 no.1
"to be led" *Whetstone* Fall 94
"hope chest" *Whetstone* Fall 94
"girl market at Gaina" *Contemporary Verse 2* Winter 93/94, 16:3
"Fashion Statement" *Contemporary Verse 2* Spring 93, no.20
"padding" ("in essays and reports") *Contemporary Verse 2* Fall 89, vol.11 no.4
"(for my brother)" *Women's Education des femmes* Sep89, vol.7 no.3
"On the occasion of your Ph.D." *The Mattawa Chronicle* Fall 88, vol.1 no.1
"burn victim" *Canadian Author & Bookman* Summer 88, vol.63 no.4
"now you want..." ("now that there's AIDS") *Bite* Spring 88, no.4
"electronic studio" *Contemporary Verse 2* Winter 88, vol.11 no.1
"rondo" *Ariel* Apr87, vol.18 no.2
"fire, for phil" *Whetstone* Fall 86
"to paul" *Whetstone* Spring 83
"counterpoint" *Whetstone* Fall 82
"hayride" *Tower* Summer 82, vol.31 no.1
"this is the season" *Whetstone* Spring 81
"solitude on the steppes" *Whetstone* Spring 82
"crucifixion" *Whetstone* Spring 82
"down a hollow" *Interior Voice* Winter 81/82, no.1
"distance softens" *Canadian Author & Bookman* Spring 81, vol.56 no.3
"youth" *Mamashee* Winter/Spring 81, vol.4

Thanks to Shirley Gould for "to be led"

solitude on the steppes

i wake	3
four grown human beings	5
later in the evening	6
burn victim	7
i hurl my screams	8
solitude on the steppes	9
down a hollow	10
Portrait of the Artist, Struggling	11
youth	12
this is the season	13
Sonata for the Dead	14
dreaming of kaleidoscopes	17

i chirp

canary in a cave	21
we move	22
nuns	23
In An Art Gallery	24
Vinnie	25
my pet parrot	26
it's like a hunger strike	28
Blacks founded great empires	29
Gameboy	30
Desert Storm (the video)	32
you tell me about your son	33
(Blind) Lady of Justice	34
tanka	35

counterpoint

you will wash over me	39
Aria Cantabile	40
no	47
your words scrape across my skin	48
counterpoint	49
a rush of flames	50
distance softens, darkness too	51
to paul	52
leave	53
Modern Math	54
to phil	57
we who have cast off polite camouflage	58

for my brother

in the night	61
now that there's AIDS	62
"rape with a foreign object"	63
electronic studio	64
evolution	65
crease, flip, crease, flip, crease, flip	66
for my brother	67
To My Philosophy Professors	69
in essays and reports	70
to be led	71
Fashion Statement	72
I have taken vows	73
Crucifixion	74
when her mother explained	76
agèd women waiting	77
Mirrors in a Funhouse	78
The Girl Market at Gaina	79
On the Occasion of your Ph.D.	80

solitude on the steppes

i wake

i wake.
the sky is like soiled snow at a spring sewer.
there are tears in the air.
every morning we leave the apartment
they go to work, i go to school.
we walk along streets
hearing the ebb and wash of the tide of traffic
as it sterilizes the pavement with carbon monoxide.
they go to buildings
that do not scrape the smog from the sky.
i go to a displeasing dome
by dubious decree.

and then sometimes for supper
we go to McDonalds.

and i remember
sitting in class
my gaze caught upon a cocoon
up there
where the ceiling is seamed
so pure and white
i felt its rough softness with my eyes
and when i saw it i dreamed
perhaps i will see
the butterfly burst out.

and i remember
for my Confirmation
auntie gave a rosary
our fathers in diamond, hail marys in pearl
so you can pray for the poor, she smiled.

when i saw it i screamed.
in embarrassment mother smiled
thank you, she is too young to understand
i will put it in a safe deposit box
until she is older.

i listen to music
upstairs in an attic
that is my room of my own now
Beethoven boasts his beating heart and
Springsteen makes me move and
no one tells me turn it down.
last night, i listened to a song called "Sunrise"
the first few bars so wakened into glory–
in the morning, this morning
i rose
and bicycled six miles out of the city,
i saw gossamer glistening,
in the silver mist,
crystal veins dripping opal,
and as i sat in an open field,
i saw the sun rise!

and i thought,
        i feel
therefore i am.

i remember hope and i remember despair
but i forget
which is the key for life–

1982

four grown human beings

four grown human beings
each half a lifetime used
sit around the table;
playing their new game of
Triple Yahtzee
because it's Christmas;
triple strategy
triple excitement
triple fun;
it says so on the box.

they sit
passing the bright shaker of dice;
talking seriously
knowingly
of the best way to win;
it matters.

the properly-dressed woman of forty-five
yells "Yahtzee!" in glee
when the dice fall right;
she carefully counts and
records her score;
she's happy now.

she turns to me and boasts
"I've had three Yahtzees this game!"
and i almost answer
i'm proud of you mom–
but i bite my tongue,
and my heart bleeds.

1976

later in the evening

later in the evening
long after dinner and dishes were done
i came again to the kitchen
and this time
saw him.
our beloved budgie who delighted
in the flat chrome top of the fridge door
hadn't turned quick enough this time
his tail caught between
and with the closing jolt
he lost his balance
flipped over the edge
to hang helpless
as he still hung now
his little birdfeet clenched
into stiff fists
his eyes bulged wide and still.
i opened the door
cupped him in my hand
and wept.

how long, i wondered–
when last did someone–
what does it feel like–

no, i need not ask about the pain
of dying
with the people you love all around
not even noticing.

1982

burn victim

i am always cutting flesh
taking from one part
to heal another–
survival of the self
sufficient.

1984

i hurl my screams

i hurl my screams!
they just strike the walls
and ricochet in hap
hazard madness
within the space of my room…
they collide, explode,
or clatter empty upon the floor
on and on
within the time of my room...
it's deafening.

no,
i know the sound of my own screams.
this room is far too quiet.

1979

solitude on the steppes

wolf wanderings
pacing to and fro
and fro and fro
silverlight on snow
g listen.

soul scavenging
contenting with fleshscraps
m eager.

sacrisufficing self.

1980

down a hollow

down a hollow
to the driftwood
strewn along my mind
my soul seeks an anchor
but finds upon the rocks
an hourglass–
crystal eggs in golden frame
shattered by the ocean
  pieces reflecting nothing in the dark
    disintegrating sandcastles drifting out

the splinters of dreams
cut.
i bleed.
and the waters redden,
          wash,
and carve the driftwood in my mind

1978

Portrait of the Artist, Struggling

unarmed i loiter at the edge of the field
casting nervous glance at shreds of flesh
still sticking to bones of those before
i falter at this fear of mediocrity
turn and dally, dally and turn
(there is hope, there is safety,
in potential, in becoming–
a battle unfought is a battle undefeated)
coward, i stall confrontation
i crawl from my anxiety into shaming naps of negligence
but awake, always, in apprehension and despair

and still, i do not dare
i do not dare

1982

youth

splashes upon a tabula rasa
berry juice and tempera
trees and knees
and Jesus and clocks
that box us in
and sin
making little black marks
upon that pure white canvas
of April snows
and the rose beneath
bequeathed in bitter
comedy
oh how tragic
the magic is
lost among the caves
and berry juice

1977

this is the season

this is the season.
i go out
stumbling through gardens gray
      dusty gossamer
           barnacled birdnests
  flowers ghosting on the fringe.

once
bundling through forests fey
i felt gilded treebark and
chipmunks giggling and

  a falling leaf touched my hair.

1981

Sonata for the Dead

I Largo

thus i begin
my long sonata for the dead
upon my instrument
this unstrung bass i play
a dirge in the minor mode.

to choose
   between
either or
yes no
to make that leap
or huddle, quivering
at every door

to live can only be to die
gripping the taper
i fury as it flickers, fades
the glass of water
half empty half
is still there
in spite of all.

evaporating.

II Minuet and Trio

i'm told
the minuet adds a stately grace to the sonata.
in corsets and crinolines and cummerbunds
there is no state of grace
to be had
by jellied rosaries.

the world is full of
unanswered prayers
Bruckner's
   Hagar's
      van Gogh's
mine.

but we dance
we twitch in two-four time
(festering beetles all of us)
trying to find the pattern,
the pulse.

(there is no trio
neither divine nor diabolic.
remember the plagal cadence is not authentic.)

III Rondo

still winter
shroudy skies
in the mourning

still mourning
dawn dribbles through curtained pain
seeps into puddle on sill
evaporating

still evaporating
crusts upon my bed
i'm holding on to mould
and whimpers of immortality
i twitch

still twitching
i crawl around the wasteland of my life
around the wasteland
around the waste

still waste
shall i end with a tierce de picardie?
do i dare?
do i care.

still?

yes.

                                                1982

dreaming of kaleidoscopes
(thanks to chris)

whirls a storm
  of scarlet and crimson
     the cobweb drips
    and black and blue

black blue shrouds
   the bleeding petals
      torn
       ragged
scabs and scars
     blowing across the snow

desert voices
in a white room
stark and naked
   i
     walk slowly

twisted grey and sometimes purple
rarefied and far too dense
i walk
   i walk
      and every now

and then
   i pick up a piece
like shards of glass
      some mirrors
and i don't know
    if i throw it away
    if i lose it
    if i store it for sustenance
        to inflict
        to understand
          who.

who.

standing on a cliff
in a silent blizzard
  crumbling
and dreaming of kaleidoscopes
all the pieces always fit

and i don't know
  i won't take the one with the sharpest edge
and make the cut
to end all cuts.

                                                          1984

i chirp

canary in a cave

i see shadows on the wall
of things happening beyond me.

petrified into paralysis
by too much and too little,
i sit in the dark

and chirp.

1983

we move

    we move

                                      with

                                          wooden

                spasms

  marionettes

          with

                              umbilical

                                        strings

1985

nuns

nuns
  habits of black and white
explaining their faith

1984

In An Art Gallery

tourists through life
posing with Rodin
for a photo
of their vanity

1978

"All I would ask would be that people do not meddle with me when I am busy painting, or eating, or sleeping, or taking a turn at the brothel, since I haven't a wife."

                                                      van Gogh

Vinnie

my idol
my starry starry night
my symbol of the misunderstood
you are all too easy
to understand.
i've looked at each painting
i've read every letter:
it is a portrait of a young man
as a commercial artist.

you're not trying hard enough to sell
my pretty flowers and sceneries,
you scold your brother as he supports you
too incompetent or too greedy or too selfish
to support yourself, to support your own art.

and that bit with the ear–
the madness of genius?
hardly.
a childish tantrum is more likely
or the madness of syphilis.

1992

my pet parrot

my pet parrot
was kidnapped
taken from its home
its family and friends
taken by force
by net, lasso, or glued stick
i'm sure it squawked and screeched
in protest, in panic
viciously pecking
struggling, bright emerald feathers flapping, breaking
to no avail–
rammed into a cage too small.

i imagine it trapped
puffing and hissing
trying to stay balanced
with each unseen bump
in the road
trying to survive decompression
in an aircraft hold
i imagine it huddled
alive, alone
in the far corner of that cramped cage
crying, as parrots do
trying to dream of rain and forests
haunted by nightmares instead
of endlessly cackling for a cracker
i imagine it pecking at itself
plucking its green plumage gone dull
tearing at itself
hearing the cries of the hundreds stacked
kidnapped the same way

i imagine it staring straight ahead
breathing too fast
the foul air of blood, shit, and fear
wondering what next
waiting anxiously

to be sold

to me.

1992

"Each year, due to an unexplained phenomenon known as stranding, entire families of whales and dolphins attempt to beach themselves on Canadian shores and die devastating and preventable deaths."

Green Living

it's like a hunger strike

it's like a hunger strike, you assholes
or dousing ourselves with gasoline
then lighting a match
it's a protest, a media thing
understand?
it would take too long
to teach you our language,
understand?

do you understand?

1992

Blacks founded great empires

Blacks founded great empires–
but of course you've never heard of
Ghana, Mali, and Songhay

Before the Europeans came
life in Africa was as advanced
as that in Europe

The first Black immigrants
to the U.S.A.
were *not* slaves

We were with Pizarro in Peru
Cortes in Mexico, Menendez in Florida–
a Black founded Chicago

We were at Bunker Hill, Valley Forge
Abilene and Dodge City–

hard to believe
black can be so invisible:
it's the first thing you notice
when you see me

1992

gameboy

i saw my son the other day
playing with one of those gameboy things
i asked him where he got it
he said he bought it
with his birthday money and saved allowance
so i let him be
his dedication was admirable

though i was awful curious about the key at the side
silver and shiny like on a wind-up toy
gameboys usually don't have those, do they?
it's a new model, my daughter explained
you have to move up through levels
just like before
but the last level activates the key
and what does it do, i asked
dunno, she said, don't care

but my son did, it was clear
he was addicted
put it down for a while, will you?
he ignored me
how do you get from level to level?
he ignored me
by following the instructions, she said, bored,
correctly and quickly

well that's pretty lame, i said
son, listen to me for a minute–
he wouldn't listen
he kept right on playing
and in no time at all
he reached the last level
we could tell by the look on his face

and when the thing commanded
TURN KEY NOW
he did
and the thing said
CONGRATULATIONS–
YOU HAVE JUST DESTROYED THE PLANET.

1992

Desert Storm (the video)
(only $19.95 from J-Tel order now)

i thought snuff films were illegal in this country.

1991

you tell me about your son

you tell me about your son
finally discharged
after three years

and i think of an institution for the mentally ill

you say then,
he was in the army

i shrug–
same thing.

1992

(Blind) Lady of Justice

we were talking about war and sports
and the whole double standard thing about violence–
it's okay if you're in a uniform:
a uniform legitimizes, i say
it anonymizes, you say at the same time

we stop
wondering if they're the same

wondering why they're the same

wondering who put the blindfold
on the Lady of Justice

1988

tanka

more terrifying
than Hiroshima victims
whose eyes have melted
is the awful knowledge that
it will not move me to act

1983

counterpoint

you will wash over me

you will wash over me
    like the waves of the sea
        till the stones in my heart
            turn to sand
there you will build castles
    in the sun
        and the wind...

–but the moon changes
and the night–

        ...then as the tide rushes in
    it recedes
leaving shells along my shores
        that hold nothing
    but the sound
of you

1979

Aria Cantabile

I

is this the way it is to be then?
         no farewell?
                 no see you soon?

i still watch the moon and wonder.

II

i grasp
  and clutch
  the bleeding roses.
you hurl me aside
       and i lay alone
            cast upon my virgin snow.
but it's my april
  let me love!
why can't you love me
    as you love all that is living
            i am living, look, damn it!
     i breathe
i bleed.

the piercing thorns remind me so.

III

an art–
   to reconcile two realities–
the intangible conceives
the tangible must create.

  i fantasysoar
        choreography scored
    by the sound alone:
reflections, in the studio mirror,
a toad caught in motion.
    i have read Shelley through
        left ope the casement
     for Erato's breath:
and still i write
these high school lines.

and you.
   upon my soulscape
        i have touched
oh i have touched–
   a child, discovering,
your brow, your cheek,
     in the candledark
   the prelude of our eyebeams
            reaching out
       intermingling
   and merging adagio our mouths
seeking, hungrily, sought.
   trembling your touch
       upon my face, my neck
  flowing along the sands of shape
a sculptor, knowing.
     exploring gently
        probing then finding
–a quick breath at the dormant quickened–

       finding again
    and again
          rising as you enter,
               crescendo, climax.
        and ah, the floatfall after
     into warmth, washing
  between the spaces not there
      between
   us.
upon my soulscape
so have i touched.

overwhelmed with the strains of song
     why can't the words be written well.
ah, the strains–
  we played a presto
       perhaps therein lies our fault
  or we, singing in dubious melody
        expected instant harmony.
caught again in our hopes, our dreams,
we silence the screams that will not be mute.
     our eyes tell.
we found the cadence imperfect.
                             you left.
before the piece was through.
  and i lay alone, a piece, through.
dissonance unresolved.

        there may be a perfect close
     or yes, perhaps, deceptive.
   we must let the music play.
string the lute, let the fires be lit,
a pas-de-deux may still be tried.

IV

amidst a winter collapse:
   heavy clouds had long shrouded
      starry, starry nights.
     wandering along those fields of waste
   cold snow packed my lungs
i could not breathe
i could not believe
i could, not.
   dreams deferred so long
they were scabbèd skeletons
    hanging
  in the sanctums of my soul.

then a spring miscarried:
   i waited years, yes years
     to love body with soul
   but touches, tears,
  you couldn't stay with me
wouldn't lay with me
     all through the night.
you knew my need
  before i knew your greed.
    and i doubted myself once more
once more the hollow woman.

(naive, Miranda believed.
  a novice no longer
    hurt burns into anger
      anger smolders into bitterness
Ophelia knew.)

V

go then.

exposed by foil
i am coward
   afraid to risk
      too full of doubts and wayward wonders.
i am the small pretender
calling myself poet.
    i would be parasite
   soul-leech to your strength.

go then.
give all to your art.
and be great.

VI

your art?
   your sterile passion! your egocentric obsession!
      god it sickens me.
Your Art.
   it exists at the expense of others
     if that isn't Art for Art's Sake, what is?
you're a cliché!

No, you cry
   Art for the sake of the Objective Truth!

oh,
  then,
     perhaps i can.
        perhaps i can climb onto your altar
–but do you know? couldn't it be?
   Art for the sake of the Subjective Scrawl.

VII

you make me strong
and you make we weak.
    i look at you
        and think i can.
   then i hear you
and know i can't.
      and when i touched you
           i–

VIII

i have leapt
  into the whirling pool
i have passed through
      the Centre of Indifference
    again, again,
and again the extremities
     of each turning circle–
either the Everlasting Yea
or the Everechoing No.

tired, i have wept.

IX

    i am not asking
       come live with me and be my love
i too must
demand damned solitude.
 yet,
   being a lone, alone
dives
dark

deep
into the abyss.
   and sometimes,
       another voice,
           another hand,

these words have become flesh
   look! they bleed upon the page
     pulsating
bright red against the grey.

                                     1982

no

no,
i shall never be totally devoted
         totally dedicated,
    to anything
again.

once capable of conviction
far beyond the human norm
a single deception
spilled doubt upon my soul
like a stain.

1981

your words scrape across my skin

your words scrape across my skin
      nerve-strings recoil, stretch, twist
    trying to phrase a melody
                   trying to
wrench beauty from truth.

                          1983

counterpoint

two lines of melody
refusing to coincide
collide
again and again
with each beat
they twist and tangle
leaving all my notes
in knots

1982

a rush of flames

a rush of flames
at the core
and all of me is melting, down
there's nothing left
but the hot liquid
in a pool upon the floor

soon,
i'll harden.

1978

distance softens, darkness too–

distance softens, darkness too–
but only for those who look, it seems.
a mountain still feels hard at night
and colder.

so as we lie, soft and warm,
only looking at love, at dreams–
whenever will we dare to feel
the glaciers
and gouged flesh.

1979

to paul

no more shall i quiver
as our eyebeams twist and threat
upon one double string–
you have made me too aware
such conversation is in the ear of the beholder.

winds no longer whisper
waves do not reassure–
that is personification
a literary technique
a pathetic fallacy.

the moon was once a marbled orb–
now it is pockmarked
with named craters.

my music is not the voice of my soul–
it is organized sound
synthesized by neurons.

and if some gypsic minstrel should beckon
come live with me and be my love
i shall have to answer
it is too late–
my passions are but chemicals
bleeding through my brain.

1981

leave

leave.
a decision.

sever.
quickly done.

but as i walk away
each fine tendril drags out slowly
back through its burrow
(mined through the days and years and effort and love-)
singeing exposed nerves at each millimetre
        pulling
      retreating
    extracting

leaving.

and finally,
the fibres dangle
tingling,
   twitching at the harsh cold air
then,
lifeless,

1980

Modern Math

1.

lines for my love

unlike those in relation parallel'd
we two are as lines intercepting:
therefore, covering more, we are close less,
yet, our separate distances upon the other
do not depend for measure,
and our facility to direction change
rests, perhaps, unparallel'd;
so let us love our intercepting lines
forgetting not that parallels
in touching doth self-negate.

2.

1 + 1 =
it depends:
there's so much to consider:
i mean sometimes it equals 2

but what if one of them is negative
then you end up with nothing at all

and in base one
it equals 11

and anyway
perhaps the more important question is
what is 1 + 1
greater than

or less than

3.

why is the circle
the symbol of love?
  because it's never-ending
so is the square–

and it has corners to hide in.

4.

the shortest distance between two points
is not a straight line–
it is a line that detours around dreams
lest it get caught or confused
in their multicoloured spirographics
and either change direction or never come out,
it is a line that encloses broken promises
with the deliberation of an etch-a-sketch
before moving on,
it is a line that arcs around conflict
and crisscrosses over canyons of pain,
no, the shortest distance between two points
is not a straight line–
it is a line of curving tangents
that never connects

5.

they say the line is an illusion:
solid, continuous–
it is only points, here and there, seen together
make it seem so

how appropriate, therefore,
that we sign today
on a dotted line

6.

we were binary
an ordered pair of single values
and even as we grew complex
each of us a string of values
for a long time
we were even an identity

but then
exhausted by the conflicts of range and domain
  frustrations of circular functions
delusions of rational and transcendental functions
i attempted transformation–

but it always stayed the same.
through translation, rotation, reflection
it was always still the same thing, really.
but then what can you expect from
such rigid motions?

so i stretched, and sheared,
mapping myself into new territory
–you didn't even notice the ellipse–
                        broke open a bit
and found myself a perfect parabolic!

(i dream of hyperbolas
of becoming two by myself
each curve extending into infinity)

1992

to phil

once
misunderstanding my fascination with flame
i saw myself moth
dusty descendent of maggot
fluttering blinded to your light.

later
i flew to you as firefly
misbelieving i recognized kin
in your intermittent flashes.

now
i burn alone, taper
dying as i live
at peace with my passion
and phoenix.

1981

we who have cast off polite camouflage

we who have cast off polite camouflage
dare to move in undressed desire;
sleek and restless in our naked need,
we slip through social labyrinths
crammed and crowded with stiff costume,
easy in urgent search for kin, we seek.
perchance we collide or coincide:
in our fugitive couplings we grapple and clutch
desperate flesh screaming from the heat
leaps pulsing into exultation–
stilled, slaked, we lay then,
we who are free,
laughing.

1982

for my brother

in the night

in the night, your mouth at my neck
a long passionate kiss arches my back
then stronger, hungrier, more purposeful–
i wonder how close you are to my jugular
do you mean to suck at my core?
but you stop
and i am still alive
so i think of leeches instead of vampires.

the next morning, i stand at the mirror
from behind you wrap your arms around me
i am looking at my neck
and seeing the truth of your intent:
a territorial claim to ownership.
then i look at your face and see more
the arrogant leap from brand to birthmark.

during the day, someone asks about it
and realizing the truth of accomplishment
i turn and say to you
it is merely a bruise,
and therefore, nothing permanent.

1985

now that there's AIDS

now that there's AIDS
now you want to use a condom
now when it's *your* life that's at stake–
all this time, all these years
when it's been *my* life
when there was a risk of screwing up *my* life
    (it would've changed forever,
    whatever i decided–
    to abort, and suffer the anguish
    before and how long after,
    or to give it up, and know forever
    she or he was out there somewhere,
    or to keep it, and give up instead
    my own life)
you'd say no we don't need one
it feels better without one
you've got cream and an IUD and the pill
    (yeah and they all feel just great–
    the bleeding, the cramps, the headaches,
    the depression, the nausea,
    the increased risk of death
    from a blood clot or cancer,
    the chances that it won't work
    –all of that feels real good)

now you want to advertise them all over the place
now you want to take them into the classrooms
now you want to test them more rigorously
because *now, your* life is at stake
now you want to use a condom

1987

"rape with a foreign object"

i've always liked that one
i mean an unwelcome dick
is about as foreign an object
as you're going to get, no?

1987

electronic studio

it's getting so i can't work:
every time i patch a connection
i'm reminded of confinement, restraint,
bondage, forced entry–

holding the plug
    –any plug, they're all the same,
    RCA, quarter-inch, mono, stereo,
    all little silver phalluses
    visibly active, everywhere–
i move toward the jack
    –any jack, they too are all the same,
    input, output, mic, headphone,
    all fixed vaginas, immobile,
    necessarily passive, in their units–

    (oh i know why it's like this:
    the female part is stationary
    instead of the male
    because it has more energy, more power–
        but this knowledge only makes it worse.)

unable to rape
i stand there, unconnected,
without any sound.

1986

evolution

i wince to hear the sudden yowl, that feline scream
i was never convinced was the sound of orgasmic ecstasy
and i know now how the hair on a tom's cock
has evolved into tiny bristles
growing backwards from tip to shaft
so they tear at the walls
as he pulls out
when he is through:
no puss will *want* to pull away–
needless to say, it helps the species to survive.

some humans have gone beyond
such quantitative criteria for success.
so now it is i who have the bristles:
well-oiled by my desire
they are but tendrils
to tickle you as you come;
but otherwise,
the barbs will puncture, pierce,
incise streaks along your prick–
needless to say, you will never again
come this way.

1986

crease, flip, crease, flip, crease, flip

crease, flip, crease, flip, crease, flip,
i fold the kleenex into an accordion
then tie it with a tiny piece of string
(it's important to tie it right in the middle–
i have the strings all ready–)
then i separate
(don't pull it)
ply by ply
(it must be done carefully–
the layers are so thin–
they tear easily–)

IT'S BORING
AND TEDIOUS
AND STUPID

i pretend to fluff it up
as if it's something important, something artistic
then i toss it into the large flat box

WE HAVE BEEN AT THIS FOR THREE NIGHTS
my mother and i
my sister's getting married

and my brother's upstairs
allowed to do his homework
instead

i feel again those tears
of frustration and injustice

and reach for another kleenex

1987

(for my brother)

I

with a grunt of irritation
you condescend to be interrupted
and move your chair back a bit
so i can crawl
under your desk
(the one dad built special for you
now that you're at university)
so i can dust the baseboards
as is my job
(i've already done the rest of your room)

i'm quiet
careful not to disturb
because it's hard stuff, important stuff
you're doing
(i'm still only in high school
but you're at university now
it must be harder
you're getting only 60s)
i turn around in the cramped space
on my hands and knees
and see your feet

i think about washing them

i think about binding them

II

the guidance counsellor pauses
then discourages
"philosophy's a very difficult field"
and i thought

(no, not then, later)
i thought, she's telling the kid
who has the top marks in the school
it's too difficult?

III

it's true
i just find it easier
besides, compared to business
philosophy is such a bird course

no, that's a lie:
i'm smarter
and i work harder–
while you're out with your friends
friday nights
i'm at work
because *my* summer job didn't pay enough
to cover the whole year
and while you're watching tv
i'm at work
(at ten o'clock
after six hours of lectures
and just as many of typing and filing)
i move the set
so i can crawl
into the corner
to dust the baseboards
you lean and yell in irritation
because i'm in your way

because *i'm* in *your* way

1987

To My Philosophy Professors

Why didn't you tell me?
When I was all set to achieve *Eudamonia*
　through the exercise of Right Reason,
When I was eager to fulfil my part
　of the Social Contract,
When I was willing, as my moral duty,
　to abide by the Categorical Imperative
When I was focussed on Becoming,
　　through Thesis and Antithesis to Synthesis–

Why didn't you correct me?
Tell me that Aristotle didn't think I had any reason,
That according to Rousseau,
　I couldn't be party to the contract,
That Kierkegaard believes I have no sense of duty
　because I live by feeling alone,
That Hegel says I should spend my life
　in self-sacrifice, not self-development,
That Nietzsche thinks I'm good for pregnancy
　and that's about it–

Why didn't you tell me I wasn't included?

(Perhaps because you too had excluded me
　from serious consideration;
Or did you think I wouldn't understand?)

(I do.　　　I do understand.)

1987

in essays and reports

in essays and reports
we call it padding–

    i wonder why
    the fact of padded bras
    was more public
    than the fact of padded shoulders

    (i never knew men's suitcoats were padded
    until i bought one myself)

    it's funny about women's fashions:
    padded bras went out
    about the same time
    padded shoulders came in
    or vice versa

–filling in for uncertainties.

1987

to be led

to be led
by a man

to not be able to see
where i'm going

to travel backwards

        no wonder i could never learn to dance

        1987

Fashion Statement

i've always wondered about
women's garments that do up the back:

designed by men for men?
for an embrace that can undress?
behind our backs, without our knowledge?
or easy resistance?

i strain, and reach, arching my back (is that it?)
but i can't quite get that button, that zipper
so like a child (is that it?)
i must ask someone else (you?)
to help me get dressed

hospital gowns also do up the back.

so do straitjackets.

1992

I have taken vows

I have taken vows
 of obedience
  and poverty
   and (modified) chastity–
I have said
I do.

1987

Crucifixion

Tirzah Lewin
1806-1883

children born
1829
1831
1833
1834
1834
1836
1838
1839
1841
1843
1844
1846
1848
1850

from twenty-three to forty-four
the supposed prime
you were bearing children, tending children,
    bearing children, tending–
led by the lies your Father told you
of wifely duties, the sacred family,
    the blessing of motherhood

nine-month Calvaries, fourteen times
carrying a barbed cross
dead wood *and* live flesh
the burden of your belly
with aching back, swelling legs

fourteen times tied down
sweating, wrenching
with the lashes of labour

fourteen times
bleeding lamb on the altar
old maids playing High Priest

the stone doesn't fool
this epitaph is for 1829.

1981

when her mother explained

when her mother explained
what a hope chest was
she didn't know
whether to laugh or cry

1985

agèd women waiting

agèd women waiting
>   for some enchanted evening

like granite statues in a graveyard.

1981

Mirrors in a Funhouse
or
On the increased availability of abortion
for those involved in the revolution

you're not allowed to kill
unless
it's in order to kill

killing is murder
only when
it's illegal

your choice is irrelevant
unless
you choose to serve our purpose

one of them dead
is more important than
one of us alive

you're not allowed to kill
unless
it's in order to kill

1987

The Girl Market at Gaina

there's something very tired about my response
as i read of the girls
who display themselves
beside their father's livestock
for sale
to whichever of the strange men
shopping up and down
decides to buy her,
who packs up and goes then
to wherever he lives,
and who vows, on the sap of a tree
never to leave him.

nevertheless i ask again:
what the hell is this article doing
in the *Travel* section?

1992

On the Occasion of your Ph.D.

in a one-lined P.S.,
as if it only marginally concerned me–
of course i'm a bit bitter:
five years
i was with you
close to you
trying hard
supporting
and now i'm not there for the celebrations
or for the thanks
    because i left
    three years ago

        but you probably don't even recognize
        my contribution
        –you never did
        (isn't that why i left?)

        you were surprised when i told you
        i was surprised you were surprised
        –no i wasn't
        (isn't that why i left?)

years later, reflecting on the relationship
i realize how typical:
the woman caring about, worrying about, its future
trying always to figure out what went wrong and why
trying to mend it, make it work, make it survive
and the man
going about his business
oblivious
to the ill-health
and impending death

as it happens
i read an article about the greenham women,
or helen caldicott, or katya komisaruk,
after i read your letter–
and i suddenly see it:
the banality of it

the horror of it.

1987